Tech 2.0

World-Changing Social Media Companies

Snapchat®

by John Csiszar

Tech 2.0

World-Changing Social Media Companies

Facebook®

Instagram®

Reddit®

Snapchat®

Twitter®

WhatsApp®

Tech 2.0 World-Changing Social Media Companies

Snapchat®

by John Csiszar

Mason Crest

Mason Crest
450 Parkway Drive, Suite D
Broomall, PA 19008
www.masoncrest.com

Series ISBN: 978-1-4222-4060-1
Hardback ISBN: 978-1-4222-4064-9
EBook ISBN: 978-1-4222-7731-7

First printing
1 3 5 7 9 8 6 4 2

Produced by Shoreline Publishing Group LLC
Santa Barbara, California
Editorial Director: James Buckley Jr.
Designer: Patty Kelley
www.shorelinepublishing.com
Cover photograph by Katie Buckley.

Library of Congress Cataloging-in-Publication Data
Names: Csiszar, John, author. Title: Snapchat / by John Csiszar.
Description: Broomall, PA : Mason Crest, 2018. | Series: Tech 2.0 : world-changing social media companies | Includes bibliographical references and index.
Identifiers: LCCN 2018001249| ISBN 9781422240649 (hardback) | ISBN 9781422240601 (series) | ISBN 9781422277317 (ebook)
Subjects: LCSH: Instant messaging--Juvenile literature. | Internet industry--Juvenile literature. | Computer scientists--United States--Biography--Juvenile literature.
Classification: LCC TK5105.73 .C85 2018 | DDC 384.3/3065--dc23 LC record available at https://lccn.loc.gov/2018001249

QR Codes disclaimer:

You may gain access to certain third party content ("Third-Party Sites") by scanning and using the QR Codes that appear in this publication (the "QR Codes"). We do not operate or control in any respect any information, products, or services on such Third-Party Sites linked to by us via the QR Codes included in this publication, and we assume no responsibility for any materials you may access using the QR Codes. Your use of the QR Codes may be subject to terms, limitations, or restrictions set forth in the applicable terms of use or otherwise established by the owners of the Third-Party Sites. Our linking to such Third-Party Sites via the QR Codes does not imply an endorsement or sponsorship of such Third-Party Sites, or the information, products, or services offered on or through the Third-Party Sites, nor does it imply an endorsement or sponsorship of this publication by the owners of such Third-Party Sites.

CONTENTS

KEY ICONS TO LOOK FOR

Words to Understand: These words with their easy-to-understand definitions will increase the reader's understanding of the text, while building vocabulary skills.

Sidebars: This boxed material within the main text allows readers to build knowledge, gain insights, explore possibilities, and broaden their perspectives by weaving together additional information to provide realistic and holistic perspectives.

Educational Videos: Readers can view videos by scanning our QR codes, providing them with additional educational content to supplement the text. Examples include news coverage, moments in history, speeches, iconic moments, and much more!

Text-Dependent Questions: These questions send the reader back to the text for more careful attention to the evidence presented here.

Research Projects: Readers are pointed toward areas of further inquiry connected to each chapter. Suggestions are provided for projects that encourage deeper research and analysis.

Series Glossary of Key Terms: This back-of-the-book glossary contains terminology used throughout this series. Words found here increase the reader's ability to read and comprehend higher-level books and articles in this field.

Introduction

According to linguistic experts, human communication first began about 500,000 years ago. Written symbols were developed about 30,000 years ago. While advancements were made over the following millennia, changes evolved at a glacial pace until the information age. Smartphones, the internet, SMS, cloud computing, and other developments have ushered in a new age of communication, where images and messages can be stored and retrieved forever. So, what place would a messaging service that self-deletes communications after 24 hours have in the modern era of unlimited data storage in the cloud?

As it turns out, a major one—and it goes by the name of Snapchat.

Snapchat is a messaging service that sends multimedia messages referred to as "snaps." While originally a text-only application, the platform expanded to image sharing in December 2012 and added functions as it exploded in popularity. The idea of a real-time, "in-the-moment" app brings a sense of immediacy that attracts millennials, who are the primary users of Snapchat. In the era of the 24-hour news cycle and constant availability of various forms of media, Snapchat arrived on the technological scene to fill one of the few remaining "holes."

Snapchat is groundbreaking technology because it takes something as old as humanity itself—communication—and moves it in a new direction. The very nature of Snapchat is at once both technologically advanced and sort of "backward." It appeals to our deep desire to be in touch, to communicate, to share. Snapchat differs from other forms of social media in that its entire focus is on fleeting encounters, moments in time that rather than being captured forever are shared, celebrated, and then abandoned as users move on to the next moment.

Snapchat capitalized on its uniqueness by launching as a mobile-first company. By comparison, many developing nations skipped a traditional, wired landline, and jumped immediately into relying on smartphones and mobile technology. Snapchat moved along a similar path. The app went directly to its users, delivering an experience that came straight to their hands and pockets, instead of a computer screen. Rather than **moving** to mobile, as nearly every company before had to do, Snapchat *has always been* a mobile app.

Snapchat has never forgotten its roots in mobile communications.

And what was the connection that made Snapchat so easy to use? The answer was in the smartphone camera. While cameras used to be a "bonus" feature of early-generation mobile phones, now phones are sold and marketed based on the quality of their cameras. With quality smartphone cameras being used to capture everything from beautiful sunsets to restaurant meals, they serve as a natural path to a social media app like Snapchat. The connection is in fact so strong that Snapchat CEO Evan Spiegel even described his own company as primarily a camera company!

The bottom line is that Snapchat serves as a lens, both literally and figuratively, into the lives of its users. The app makes the world a smaller place by bringing adventures and experiences immediately across a web of interconnected individuals, who share a moment, add to it if they desire, and then move on to the next one.

But what is Snapchat, really? How does the technology behind the system work? What needs does it fulfill? What do users find exciting about it, and what's around the corner for this innovative technology? Here's a look at all the ins and outs of Snapchat, from its founding through its development and growth all the way to the current day. Even if you're a frequent user of the service, you may be surprised as to what went into Snapchat and how it has transformed a generation.

1

The Founding

The legend of Snapchat's origin is straight out of the Silicon Valley playbook—brainy university students come up with an idea in their dorm room and launch "the next big thing" in the tech world, as Facebook did. Of course, the truth is a bit murkier. Yes, Snapchat co-founders Bobby Murphy (right in photo), Reggie Brown, and Evan Spiegel (left in photo) were students together at Stanford University. Yes, they tried to invent something "cool" that would be a big hit. And yes, there was controversy surrounding one of the founders—Reggie Brown—who ultimately ended up suing the company. But there's a lot more behind the story, including the interesting background of the man in charge of Snapchat, Evan Spiegel.

WORDS TO UNDERSTAND

contentious angry, argumentative

crew a sport using long, thin rowboats pulled by two to eight athletes using a single oar apiece

venture capital money provided by investors to young companies in hope of helping them grow

war chest slang term for a huge stockpile of money that can be used to expand or grow a company

The Founders

Spiegel grew up in the wealthy Pacific Palisades area of Los Angeles, and he's not shy in sharing that his upbringing gave him a leg up in the business world. Siegel's parents, both attorneys, divorced when he was just 17, at which time court documents recorded that he requested $2,000 per month in living expenses. Spiegel claims that family connections allowed him to go to Stanford, where he rubbed elbows with future Silicon Valley tech leaders and other influential people. At a conference in 2013, Spiegel attributed part of his good fortune and success simply

Stanford University: birthplace of Snapchat (among others!).

to being a "young, educated white male," adding that "life isn't fair . . . It's not about working hard, it's about working the system." Those are just some of the comments that the colorful Snapchat head has issued over the years.

Reggie Brown attended an all-boys boarding school in Chattanooga, Tennessee, where he rowed **crew** and was an excellent student, being named a National Merit Commended Student and joining both the Cum Laude Society and the National Honor Society. He played a key role in the founding of Snapchat and also claimed credit for designing the "ghost" logo of the company, which he nicknamed Ghostface Chillah.

Bobby Murphy is the product of a Catholic education from grade school through high school, ultimately ending up at Stanford, where he met both Brown and Spiegel as a member of the Kappa Sigma fraternity. Murphy is of mixed Philippine and American heritage and received a bachelor of science degree in mathematical and computational science from Stanford before he became the co-founder and chief technology officer of Snapchat.

The three young future Snapchat moguls originally met at Stanford in 2008. By 2011, Brown and Spiegel were finishing their junior year, with Murphy already having graduated. As one version of the history goes, Brown was the one who had the original idea behind Snapchat. Spiegel thought the idea had legs, and the pair enlisted Murphy's help to write the programming for the software that was originally called Picaboo.

A Disagreement . . . and Growth

The exact truth may never be known, because the founders don't agree on it. Just one month after Picaboo launched, Brown maintains that there was a "**contentious** telephone conversation" about the future direction of the app, and that Spiegel hung up on him. According to Brown, Spiegel and Murphy stopped returning his calls, changed his passwords, and changed the name of the app from Picaboo to Snapchat.

While the drama among the founders was playing out, the budding Snapchat app was finding its footing. By April of 2012, the number of users had grown to 100,000. By May of that year,

Founding Snapchat

Jeremy Liew helped spearhead initial investment money into Snapchat.

Snapchat was already drawing interest from **venture capital** (VC) groups. One of the partners of VC Lightspeed Ventures, Barry Eggers, heard about the app the way most adults did—from kids. Eggers' teenage daughter explained to him that high school kids only used three apps: Instagram, Angry Birds, and Snapchat. Eggers shared the information with his partner, Jeremy Liew, who had heard of Angry Birds and Instagram, but not Snapchat. Liew was interested enough to follow up on Snapchat, even though the company was hard to find: Liew couldn't find any articles on the company, couldn't pull them up using a Google search, and didn't receive any response after sending an email to an address he had finally located. After some additional research, Liew unearthed Evan Spiegel's name. They were both Stanford alumni, so he sent him a message through Facebook Messenger. Having finally heard back from Spiegel, Liew set up a meeting. Although Spiegel insisted that the company wasn't looking for funding, just 10 days later, Lightspeed Ventures invested $485,000 in the company, valuing the company at $4.25 million. In 2013, the growing company—now seeing 60 million snaps sent every day—raised an additional $13.5 million in financing from a group of investors, which now placed the value of the company at about $70 million.

Investors weren't the only ones to notice that this newly formed company was doing something special. In December 2012, none other than social media giant Facebook launched its first attack at Snapchat by unveiling the "poke" feature, copying a feature that was already part of the Snapchat universe. While the idea generated a stir, it ended up backfiring on Facebook and generating lots of free publicity for Snapchat, which had just begun to spread its wings. This marked the beginning of a corporate competition that continues to this day.

On the business side of the equation, things were going incredibly well for the young Snapchat. On the legal side, however, things were unraveling rapidly. In February of 2013, shortly after Snapchat received its $70 million valuation, Reggie Brown filed a lawsuit against Snapchat. He claimed the other two founders had stolen his idea and shut him out of the company. The lawsuit was ultimately settled in September of 2014, with Brown receiving a payout of $157.5 million.

Even in the midst of its legal trouble, Snapchat continued to grow, as did its user base. The company continued innovating, rolling out new feature after new feature in an attempt to grab new users while still maintaining the interest of its core user base. With a multi-million-dollar **war chest** behind it, Snapchat had only begun its dramatic expansion.

Text-Dependent Questions

1. Which of the three founders ended up filing a lawsuit against Snapchat?

2. Which of the three founders was the brains behind the technology of Snapchat?

3. What was the original name of Snapchat?

Research Project

Snapchat raised millions of dollars in financing from investors. Each time money was raised, the company was said to have a new valuation. Research how those valuation numbers are derived based on the amount of financing received; for example, why does a $485,000 investment equate to a company valuation of $4.25 million?

2

The Development of Snapchat

Snapchat's original concept as a private, person-to-person photo-sharing app didn't last long. In rapid succession, Snapchat added the ability to send short videos (December 2012) and communicate via video chat (May 2014). Over the years, Snapchat has added a laundry list of features designed to keep its users in its own ecosystem. Part of that **ecosystem** is an entirely new vocabulary.

To fully grasp what is going on in Snapchat, users have to understand the language of Snapchat. Here's a brief rundown of important terminology in the Snapchat universe, so you'll be ahead of the game when you first download the application. (If you're already an active user, you still might learn something new):

WORDS TO UNDERSTAND

buyout an offer to pay a large sum to take over an entire company

doctored slang term for "changed" or "altered" from reality

ecosystem usually, an area of shared climate, wildlife, and resources; in this case, the environment inside the app as opposed to linking to things outside it

ephemeral having a very, very short life span; appearing only briefly

monetization the process of creating a way to make money with a product or a service

nefarious evil, criminal, dangerous

resonate connect with; be in tune with

Bitmoji: An application that allows you to create your own personalized emoji to be used as an avatar for your Snapchat sessions.

Chat: While Snapchat is primarily a photo-based service, it does have "chat" at the end of its name, and you can indeed chat via the app.

Discover: Discover provides the Snapchat user with access to outside content, provided by publishers ranging from *National Geographic* to *Cosmopolitan* who pay for the privilege. About 30

Fabulous filters quickly became a big part of Snapchat's appeal.

percent of Snapchat's revenue comes from ads in the Discover section of the app.

Filter: Filters allow you to add overlays to your snaps. You may see different filters based on where you are, what time it is, and what season you are in.

Friend List Emojis: Emojis that appear next to your friends based on how you interact with them. These are private, and they change over time based on how you interact.

Geofilter: A geofilter is a regular filter, except it is tailored to your specific location. For this feature to work, you have to give Snapchat access to your location.

Memories: Memories is the long-term storage feature for your snaps. Organized as a camera roll, you can pick and choose snaps to add to your Stories from Memories.

Snap: A snap is the fundamental "unit" of Snapchat—the basic building block of the language comprising the Snapchat universe. When you take a picture or video of yourself in the Snapchat app, you have a snap. When you send snap to a friend, it originally disappeared after 10 seconds. Now, you can set a timer between one and 10 seconds, or even longer using the infinity option. If you want to replay a snap, you have that option, but only once.

Snapcash: Snap's embedded money-transfer service that allows you to send cash to others using Square's money-transfer platform.

Snapchat Score: Your Snapchat Score keeps track of how many snaps you have sent and received.

Snapcode: Snapcodes are QR codes assigned to each user. Snapcodes make it easy to add a fellow Snapchatter simply by scanning their unique QR code, rather than worrying about user-names or email addresses.

Snapcode Selfie: A Snapcode Selfie is a way to personalize your Snapcode with your photo. If anyone looks for you in the app, they'll see the picture you post.

Snap Lenses: Lenses are like filters, allowing you to add animated special effects to your snaps; however, you use lenses while you are taking a snap, as opposed to adding filters after you've taken a snap.

Snap Map: Snapchat helps you locate and stay in touch with friends by sharing your current location on a map. When you open Snapchat, you can see where all your friends that have enabled the service are located as well. However, these features only operate

Teens turn to My Story to keep track of each other.

while you have the app open—otherwise, your most recent location while using the app will be shown.

Stories: Stories is where your snaps live—but only for up to 24 hours. You can scroll through the "My Story" section of the app to see your recent snaps and to choose which ones you want to share with your friends. If you want to see your friends' Stories, you can access them from the Snapchat camera screen by swiping left. A Story Timer counts down and lets you know how much time remains until you can no longer view an individual snap.

Streaks: A tracker that logs how many consecutive days you have interacted with another Snapchatter; streaks are "rewarded" with the granting of certain emojis.

Trophy Case: A section of the app where you can collect emojis that you earn based on certain activities that you complete. For example, you can earn the "glowing star" trophy when your Snapchat Score hits 500.

What Is the Heart of Snapchat?

Snapchat's core service is based around Stories. As a collection of your snaps, your story is your basis of interaction with others on Snapchat. You can think of Stories as a virtual camera roll that can, as the name says, tell a story. Essentially, the snaps you collect are a short-term slide show of what is going on in your life. Whether you want to share your story with others or not is up to you.

Snapchat has developed a series of features that help users tell their story. Lenses helped explode the popularity of the app starting in September of 2015. Lenses overlay your images to distort their appearance. While taking your snap, you can have rainbows shooting out of your eyes, or transform yourself into any number of crazy-looking monsters or characters. While filters were the initial exciting Snapchat overlay, lenses took filters a step beyond, allowing animated overlays instead of the static ones found in filters.

When it comes to making Snapchat addicting, there are two features that stand out in particular—friend emojis and streaks.

Friend Emojis

Friend emojis are earned via various interactions with other users. They have evolved into an important part of the Snapchat "game," as there's a certain pressure among users to maintain them once they're earned, especially those related to being best friends with another user. Here's the list of friend emojis you can earn:

• **Gold Heart:** You are best friends with this Snapchatter, since you send the most snaps to this friend and they send the most to you

• **Red Heart:** You've been best friends for at least two weeks

• **Pink Hearts:** You've been best friends for at least two months

- **Grimace:** You share a best friend with this Snapchatter
- **Smile:** One of your best friends
- **Sunglasses:** You share a close friend with this Snapchatter
- **Smirk**: You're on this Snapchatter's "best friends" list, as they send you the most snaps, but you don't return the favor
- **Baby:** You just became friends
- **Birthday Cake:** This friend is having a birthday
- **Fire:** You have a streak with this friend
- **Hourglass:** Your streak is about to end soon

Are you happy? Sad? Upset? In love? Yes, there's an emoji for that.

Streaks

For many Snapchat users, streaks are what make the app truly addicting. As referenced in the above list of friend emojis, after you've consistently Snapchatted another user for three days, you'll earn the fire emoji, accompanied by a number. This number is the amount of days that your streak with a particular friend has lasted. If you want to keep your streak alive, you have to send and

What's your record streak? See if you can do a whole year!

receive at least one Snapchat every 24 hours. If the streak is in danger of dying, the hourglass emoji appears by the other user's name. For some users, streaks become an object of obsessive devotion; if a user is going to be out of service range for a few days, for example, they might give a friend their login information so the friend can continue their Snapchat streaks until they return!

Continued Growth of Snapchat

As the new language of Snapchat began to take over smartphones around the globe, the company's fortunes were improving, as were its metrics. In 2013, Facebook approached Snapchat with a $3 billion **buyout** offer, which the company rejected. Later that year, the company raised another $50 million in investor funding, valuing the company at $2 billion.

Snapchat used that money to fight off competitor Instagram, which launched its Instagram Direct feature at the end of 2013. Instagram Direct allows users to send private messages to followers, including photos and videos, that self-delete, the same as with Snapchat. Snapchat immediately responded with additional filters, timestamps, and the ability to replay snaps, one time only.

By May of 2015, Snapchat users were sending 2 billion videos per day; by November of 2015, that number had already tripled, to 6 billion videos sent per day. By May 2017, Snapchat had 166 million daily users.

Controversy

Most groundbreaking technologies or societal changes come with their own share of controversy—and opposition. The ancient Greek philosopher Socrates warned against the dangers of *writing*, claiming it would "create forgetfulness in the learners' souls, because they will not use their memories." Rock 'n' roll music was branded the workshop of the devil; television was seen as destroying family bonds; and the internet was supposed to have negative effects on the brain.

This was once the height of technology; what will replace Snapchat someday?

Douglas Adams succinctly explained this phenomenon in his book *The Salmon of Doubt*:

"Anything that is in the world when you're born is normal and ordinary and is just a natural part of the way the world works. Anything that's invented between when you're fifteen and thirty-five is new and exciting and revolutionary and you can probably get a career in it. Anything invented after you're thirty-five is against the natural order of things."

Snapchat is the latest in a long line of innovations causing concern in society. As an app that finds its primary audience to be millennials, Snapchat doesn't **resonate** with many in older generations, who can't relate to the immediacy of the process. More controversial is the 24-hour "disappearance." In the minds of some critics, this makes Snapchat fertile ground for **nefarious** uses, ranging from inappropriate sexual content to even illegal exchanges of information. Several cases involving minors, Snapchat, and sexually abusive material have made headlines. Some parents fear that the rapid deletion of photos and other media may encourage younger users to send inappropriate material, thinking that it will vanish, when in reality, receiving users can choose to save pictures they receive, effectively making them live forever.

It's unlikely that Snapchat will change the immediacy features of the app, as they are what appeal most to its user base.

As such, parents and guardians will have to remain careful about teaching young people about the dangers of online interaction, just as they already should be teaching them regarding websites, chat rooms, or other social media.

Snapchat's Place in Social Media

To many non-users, the concept behind Snapchat can seem odd. How can a social app like Snapchat be "social" when its content is so **ephemeral**? Perhaps part of the confusion comes from the predominant social network, Facebook. Facebook has taught the world how a social network runs—users post videos, stories, or news items that are collected in a single place and last forever; users can see and comment on

Snapchat had to find a way around Facebook.

The Failure of Spectacles

It's tough to be an innovative company. In addition to inventing technology ahead of its time, to be successful, you have to bring the right product to the right market at the right time. Snapchat's Spectacles product was no doubt innovative, but the bungled release doomed it from the outset.

The idea was indeed new—Spectacles was meant to be a natural extension of the Snapchat app, placing a camera in eyeglasses to allow users to take videos in 10-second increments. However, for a company whose core product is based on immediacy, the rollout of Spectacles was remarkably slow. Snap did a great job of building hype for the product, but waited five months to roll it out to the public for mass purchase. Additionally, the company didn't provide the glasses to social media influencers who could help build sustained publicity for the product. While long lines of trendy youths showed up to buy the glasses on Venice Beach, the buzz died rapidly. Only 0.08 percent of Snapchat's users ever bought the camera glasses, and those who did hardly used them. Snap's own internal data indicated that less than 50 percent of those who bought the product were still using it even one month later, with a large percentage stopping after just one week.

Without buzz behind Spectacles, only negative product reviews seemed to fill the void. Users indicated problems with everything from the easily obstructed lens, to the lack of real-time video playback, to the camera that underperformed in low light, and no automatic uploading of videos in high-def.

Perhaps Spectacles was just ahead of its time—after all, another technology giant had its own spectacular failure years earlier with Google Glass. Perhaps Snap tried to hype a product before it was really ready to be released. It just showed that even innovators can make mistakes.

the posts forever, making Facebook a vast, long-lasting holding place for memories and stories.

Snapchat exists on another plane entirely. In fact, if you ask Snapchat users, many will make a comment along the lines of "Facebook is for old people." In fact, statistics show that the average age of a Facebook user is indeed much higher than a typical Snapchat user. In fact, of all the major social media platforms, Snapchat's users are among the youngest, with nearly 50 percent of its users being between the ages of 18 and 24. Only 16.5 percent of Facebook users are in the same demographic.

Part of the reason is the divide in how each company creates its social media world. Facebook is more of a scrapbook, a long-lasting collection of content that generates interest and commentary from a huge number of viewers, including "friends of friends" that might not even know the original poster. In Snapchat's world, news and stories are much more intimate, direct, and immediate. You can send a snap to a friend to get a quick laugh, and he or she can respond immediately with a snap with a filter or lens to get an equally immediate—and often hilarious— reaction. Snapchat has transformed the nature of communication by making it fun and in-the-moment.

To further show the differences between Snapchat and other social media, think about what you see when you go to your Facebook page. Typically, it's a newsfeed, stuffed with stories, photos, news items, and ads. When you open Snapchat, on the other hand, you open your camera. There's no overload of information. In fact, the "front door" of the platform invites you to create content rather than consume it. If you want to seek out information, you can find it deeper in the app; but your first access point is the camera. And that's another key difference—video in the Snapchat world is vertical. The quickest and easiest way to create content, whether still photos or video, is to hold up your phone and hit the camera button. Especially in the era of smartphones with giant

It's as easy as point and shoot . . . and upload immediately.

screens, this is easier and more natural than rotating your phone to the horizontal orientation, probably using two hands to do it. Snapchat has made vertical video the preferred choice because it fits into the whole Snapchat plan.

At the end of the day, Snapchat encourages its users to create authentic experiences. While filters and lenses can change the reality of the snaps you send, the short duration of snaps prioritizes real-world, "as-it's-happening" documentation. Because Facebook and Instagram photos are forever, users of those platforms tend to enhance their shots, presenting the best possible images. Snapchat focuses on the fun of a moment, with the "raw footage" style capturing an authenticity that can be lacking in

Snapchat tips and tricks

doctored photos. It's encouraging to know that if you send a snap that's an uninteresting "fail," it will be deleted in 24 hours—if you don't delete it yourself first—so you don't have to worry about it. Having the wrong moment immortalized forever doesn't sound like fun at all, and that is what Snapchat is all about.

Making Money?

While Snapchat is no doubt happy that its customers view its platform as a fun space to spend their time, the name of the game when it comes to so-called "unicorn" companies is **monetization**. That's the fancy name for creating a way to make money with something.

The key to Snapchat's future is turning users into money.

In the dictionary, monetization is the process of transforming users into streams of revenue. From the point of view of a company, monetization feels like a treacherous river rapid. For starters, no customer wants to be seen as a revenue stream rather than a user. For another, turning a "fun" app like Snapchat into a business is likely to cost the company some fans. Yet, the investors that poured millions of dollars into Snapchat expect a return on that money—and by "a return," most venture capitalists mean they want five, ten, or 20 times their money back. Growing a happy user base is a good thing, but a company can't keep losing money forever. While inventing a world-changing application and developing a platform so popular that billions of messages are sent on it every day may seem to be enough, it's not. Transforming a company from one that hemorrhages cash to one that turns a profit is tricky stuff. This is where a management team earns its pay.

Snapchat's first note about monetization came in October of

In 2015, Snapchat partnered with the NFL to show game action.

2014, when it announced that it was going to run ads to generate revenue. The company stated that it was going to ". . . try to deliver an experience that's fun and informative, the way ads used to be, before they got creepy and targeted." In that spirit, Snapchat's first ad was a 20-second movie trailer for the horror film *Ouija*.

By July of 2015, Snapchat realized that some of its core features—Snapchat filters and lenses—were potential moneymakers for the company. By licensing out some lenses and filters, Snapchat could both make money and keep its app fun for users. One of its first steps in that direction was creating a branded geofilter for McDonald's, which covered its restaurant locations across the United States. Soon after, Snapchat broadened its usage of sponsored lenses and filters. Here's a brief look at some of the highlights of Snapchat's steps towards monetization:

- In May of 2016, movie studio 20th-Century Fox marketed its film **X-Men: Apocalypse** by replacing the entire Snapchat array of lenses for a single day with characters and moments from the X-Men universe.

- In September 2015, Snapchat entered into an agreement with the National Football League to provide live stories from selected games, such as Monday Night Football and Thursday Night Football.

- In April 2016, it was the Olympics' turn, with NBC Olympics agreeing to allow stories to be featured on Snapchat in the United States. The stories offered a combination of footage from

NBC, athletes and attendees, marking the first time that NBC allowed Olympics footage to be featured on a third-party property.

• April of 2017 saw the "Snap to Store" advertising tool. Companies use geostickers to track whether customers made purchases or visited their stores within seven days of seeing a geosticker.

• In May of 2017, Snapchat launched a self-service manager for advertising, shortly followed by the Snapchat Mobile Dashboard for tracking ad campaigns in select countries.

Today, Snapchat's total revenue is distributed across four

Starting in 2016, the Olympics will all have a dedicated Snapchat channel.

broad categories: ads on Discover (30 percent), ads on Live Stories (37 percent), sponsored lenses (20 percent), and sponsored geofilters (11 percent). Going forward, Snapchat will no doubt think of new ways to generate revenue out of its massive user base. However, it will have to balance the need for profit with the desire to keep users happy.

Text-Dependent Questions

1. Name three Snapcat emojis and their meanings.

2. What large company first offered to buy Snapchat?

3. Name two large sports organizations that partnered with Snapchat.

Research Project

Read more online about the issue of Snapchat information and posts "disappearing" soon after posting. Make a pro and con chart about both sides of this issue. What are some reasons people think this is a bad idea? What are some reasons that it's a positive step in communication?

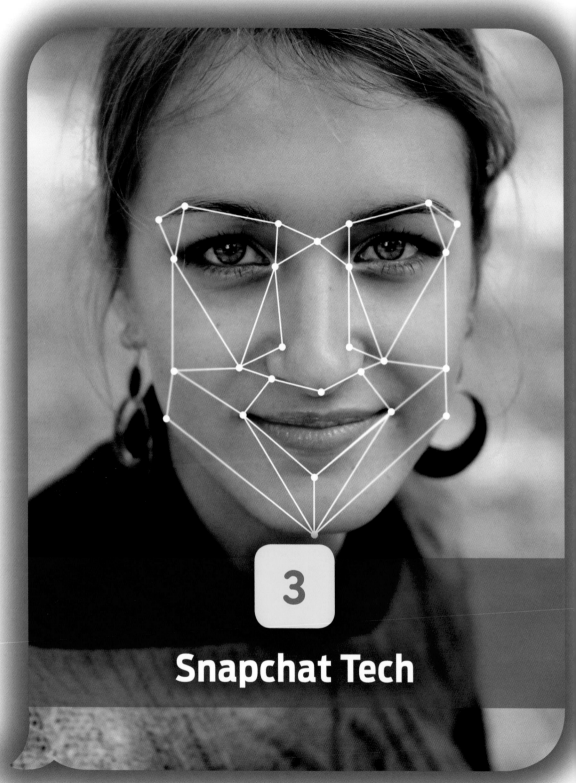

3

Snapchat Tech

ritics of Snapchat like to dismiss it as a simple photo-sharing app that transforms ordinary people into silly cartoons. The truth is, the technology behind the modern version of Snapchat is actually highly sophisticated. Snapchat's whole universe is based on a **facial recognition** engine (sample, left) made by a company called Looksery, which Snapchat bought in 2015 for about $150 million. For Snapchat's lenses to work, advanced software must do much more than simply identify a face—it has to envision a whole world around that face, in three-dimensional space. Since it's hard to keep both a human face and a smartphone still at the same time, the software has to take into account movement to properly overlay the features of any given lens. Taking that ability and applying it to a mobile device, in real time, is a fantastically advanced application.

WORDS TO UNDERSTAND

algorithm a formula or set of rules that a computer program follows

facial recognition the science of using visual cues to help a camera and a computer identify human faces and their characteristics

stack in this case, the technology term for a gathering of applications and programs connected to work in a certain area

The purchase of Looksery isn't the only technology behind Snapchat. In 2016, the company acquired Seene, a startup company with a 3D photo app, as a complement to the technology offered by Looksery. Combined, the technologies helped drive Snapchat to new directions and seem poised to dominate in the coming virtual reality world as well.

What's Behind Facial Recognition?

The Looksery technology that Snapchat relies on is fancy, but how does it actually work? Basically, all facial recognition technology is the same, relying on something known as the Viola-Jones **algorithm**. This algorithm is programmed to understand the lighting and shape of the human face.

Software combines data points to map a face.

Think of this technology as the modern version of how an artist would paint a portrait. An artist understands that it's all about shading—and so does the Viola-Jones algorithm. Some of the basic ideas behind both the

Big Brother Is Watching?

Although Snapchat's technology is impressive, privacy advocates are sounding the alarm with Snapchat as much as they are with other companies, like Facebook. The whole concept of Snapchat relies on "snaps" of real users. While Snapchat says it deletes snaps from its servers after users view them, they may still be accessible on individual devices. However, when pictures float around cyberspace, they often land places you might not expect or want them to be. The federal government already has facial recognition scans on millions of Americans. Facebook actually uses facial recognition software to scan every photo in its database, so it can tag users with names. Some privacy advocates are concerned that a program like Snapchat, which maps detailed points on users' faces to create its selfie filters, could be used for the wrong reasons. While there is no evidence that Snapchat is creating a massive database of names and faces and/or working with the federal government to keep tabs on people, the technology clearly exists for this to happen.

The other danger in allowing companies to handle large swaths of user data is the risk of cyberattack. Even Snapchat is not immune to security problems. At the end of 2013, a massive data breach exposed the usernames and phone numbers of more than 4.6 million users. Some users were concerned that the company didn't take the leak seriously. The company also had to endure a PR hassle by not immediately making apologies to users; the CEO first said that he didn't owe anyone an apology for the hack. The overall tone of the response made some wary of how Snapchat handled private user data. Ultimately, users have to make their own judgments as to how comfortable they are with companies handling data. For any app or program that requests permission to store or "snap" something personal in nature, users should be aware of the dangers.

algorithm and painting are that the bridge of the nose is always brighter than the sides of a nose, just as the center of the forehead is lighter than the sides. The eye sockets are darker still. Snapchat's technology takes the algorithm further by identifying where specific facial features begin and end. Using these beginning and ending points, the app can created a 3D scan of your entire face and overlay its filters in the appropriate places. The filters can still work even when you move because the facial scan fits like a technological glove over your image, moving and flexing as you change your position.

Under the Hood

All companies use various software programs and applications to get things done. Collectively, these programs are known as a "**stack**." Typically, companies have three types of stacks: technology stacks, for infrastructure; application stacks, for employees; and DevOps stacks, for developers. Snapchat has three divisions in its stack: application and data, utilities, and business tools. Here's a brief look at programs that Snapchat uses to keep its system up and running:

Application and Data

Android SDK (Frameworks): The Android Software Development Kit (SDK) is a set of development tools that allows programmers to write programs for Android. Typically, the Android

SDK is used with an integrated development environment that provides a graphical interface so developers can complete development tasks faster.

Objective-C (Languages): Objective-C is the object-oriented programming language behind Apple's OS X and iOS X operating systems—and Snapchat!

Google App Engine (Platform as a Service): The Google App Engine is a cloud-computing platform that allocates resources

The Objective-C language is at the heart of key operating systems.

across multiple servers. That lets clients scale. If there's a greater demand for service, no one single server gets overwhelmed.

Google Compute Engine (Cloud Hosting): The infrastructure-as-a-service portion of the Google Cloud platform, which allows users to employ virtual machines that boot quickly and deliver high-quality performance.

Semantic UI (Front-End Frameworks): A front-end, lightweight development format that uses HTML to create responsive and attractive layouts.

Cocoa Touch iOS (Frameworks): The application-development environment to build software for iOS and OS X platforms; works in conjunction with Objective-C.

Snapchat filters explained

Utilities

Google Analytics (General Analytics): Google's web analytics service that lets users track and report web traffic; currently, the most widely used web analytics service.

SendGrid (Transactional Email): A cloud-based email server; lets users send email without having to maintain servers.

The software that runs Snapchat interacts with computers and phones.

Business Tools

G Suite (Productivity Suite): The G Suite is a collection of Google tools that even non-developers are familiar with, including Gmail, Calendar, Drive, Hangouts, and more. The G Suite is cloud-based, enabling groups of co-workers to share work over video conferences, social media, real-time document collaborations, and more.

Zendesk (Help Desk): A customer service platform utilizing a suite of products to improve relationships between companies and their customers.

Zendesk is a Snapchat product like this customer service hub.

Tumblr (Hosted Blogging Platform): Tumblr is a blogging platform that allows marketers to create GIFs and other engaging materials to attract user interest.

Text-Dependent Questions

1. What is the name of the facial recognition algorithm?

2. Name and describe one of the components of the "stack" that Snapchat utilizes. What is it and what does it do?

3. Briefly describe how Snapchat's facial recognition technology works.

Research Project

Use Snapchat to make a story about your research into how the app operates. Go online and find articles that go more in depth about the technology in this chapter, then document what you find by making snaps!

4

Now and the Future

Since the beginning of its existence—and likely for the near future—Snapchat's core audience has always been millennials. The generational love of Snapchat likely stems from two main things—a familiarity with technology and a desire to live an immediate, "in-the-moment" existence. But what is Snapchat really used for?

In 2014 researchers from Seattle Pacific University and the University of Washington looked into Snapchat. They thought that the private, self-deleting nature of the messages led to "sexting" and other sexual content. The actual numbers revealed something very different. Only 14 percent of people studied admitted sending sexual content via Snapchat as some point. And only 1.6 percent said that was the app's primary use. It turned out that the study showed the opposite of what it expected. More than 74 percent of users said they were

WORDS TO UNDERSTAND

bandwagon slang term for a movement to join something after it has become big, rather than follow something throughout its rise

court woo, convince to join or connect, try to influence

shares in this case, individual pieces of a company that are bought and sold

trajectory the direction something is moving in

upstart young and aggressive new company or person

not willing to send sexual content via Snapchat. Other types of content considered "off limits" for Snapchat by users included photos of documents (85 percent), legally questionable messages (86.6 percent), or "mean" or "insulting" content (93.7 percent).

So what is the primary use of Snapchat? Humor. Nearly 60 percent of people from the study said that their most common usage of Snapchat was for sending "stupid faces." In spite of the potential for misuse of the self-deleting feature of Snapchat, the ultimate conclusion of the study was that people use Snapchat because they consider it to be fun.

A picture like this one might be the perfect example of Snapchat humor.

Everyone wants to run a fun company, but Snapchat is still a business in search of profits. While revenue has increased, the free social camera app is still not raking in big bucks. A late 2017 report showed revenue of $208 million. However, it was actually losing money, more than $400 million. That means it was spending $600 million more than it was taking in. Snapchat as a company is always looking for new ways to make its "free" app gather revenue.

Let's take a look at some of those ways and where they might be headed in the future.

Interface Redesign

In November 2017, Snapchat underwent a redesign of its "look" in an attempt to make the app easier to use. Specifically, Spiegel says that the company wants to clearly separate messages from friends and content from publishers, as ". . . your friends aren't content, they're relationships." Going forward, swiping right from the main camera screen brings users to a redesigned Discover page, and swiping left brings users to a Friends page that brings together chats and Snapchat Stories. Spiegel admitted that a newly designed "front page" could be a gamble, in that it could disrupt current users without adding additional ones. Spiegel noted that " . . . we don't yet know how the behavior of our community will change when they begin to use our updated application."

Is the Future in Gaming?

Snapchat's redesign could at least in part be tied to its relationship with a new investor. The Chinese gaming company Tencent said that it had bought 145.8 million **shares** of Snapchat in 2017, representing 12 percent of the company. The world's largest gaming company, Tencent indicated that it wanted to cooperate with Snapchat ". . . on mobile games publishing and newsfeed," including the potential for newsfeed ads. The working relationship between the two companies could be interesting on both ends. Tencent already owns the top-grossing mobile game

League of Legends maker Tencent has a competing app to Snapchat.

in the world, Honor of Kings, and it has relied on social media to help increase its popularity. Tencent also owns Riot Games, which is the developer of League of Legends, the most popular computer game in the United States and Europe.

Interestingly, Tencent—one of the largest companies in the world—also owns messaging apps QQ and WeChat, which dominate the messaging market in China. Snapchat, on the other hand, is currently banned in China, like its other social media competitors, leading some to wonder if a tie-up with a prominent Chinese company could help Snap gain entry to the massive market there.

This particular relationship is one to watch. It could grow bigger and change the future growth **trajectory** of Snapchat.

Broadening Relationship With Influencers

A social media influencer is a personality with an authentic voice and a level of credibility among social media users. A positive review or endorsement from a prominent social media personality can result in instant attention and acclaim for the subject of that review. Part of future Snapchat strategy is to get social media influencers more involved in the app. Snapchat has always been a user-first platform, but Snapchat the company has not gone out of its way to **court** specific users to use the application. While competitors provided specific tools to help influencers track their performance, Snapchat had never gone out of its way to provide this type of assistance. Snap CEO Spiegel announced in November of 2017 that this was going to change. According to Spiegel: "We have historically neglected the creator community on Snapchat. In 2018, we are going to build more distribution and monetization opportunities for these creators . . . Developing this ecosystem will allow artists to transition more easily from communicating with friends to creating Stories for a broader audience, monetizing their Stories, and potentially using our professional tools to create premium content."

Much as influencers shape trends on YouTube, a stronger influencer presence on Snapchat could open the doors to new avenues of revenue and more users for the company.

Snapchat and the future of news

IPO: "Going Public"

The stamp of success—indeed, some-times the main goal—for many new or young companies is when they "go public," meaning they sell shares of stock to the general public. After this initial public offering, or IPO, the shares trade on a stock exchange, like the New York Stock Exchange. Going public generates a tremendous financial windfall for the company, and that money is often used to grow and expand. The original investors in the company, typically including the founders, also enjoy a big payday when their company goes public.

Shares of a "hot" IPO can often spike up dramatically in price, as they did in the case of Snapchat. The company's shares were priced at $17 per share. By the end of the first day of trading, they closed at $24.48 per share, a gain of 44 percent. Everything seemed to be happening just as expected, and investors were likely giddy at the fortunes they were making in such a short time.

Unfortunately, in spite of its widespread popularity, things quickly turned south for Snapchat. By April 2018, its stock was trading more than 50 percent below the closing price of its first day, eventually falling to about $14 per share. (Stock watchers can check out the symbol SNAP on stock-market sites to see how the shares are selling now.)

Like many high-growth companies, Snapchat has been pouring money back in its business. It is trying to increase its user base and broaden its appeal with new products and services. Even with a low share price, Snapchat is still an unbridled success.

Competition

As is often the case with rapidly growing companies, success brings competition. Snapchat was the innovator when it came to the world of lenses, filters, and self-deleting messages. However, other larger, more established companies have jumped onto the **bandwagon** and represent a serious threat to the company's long-term survival. Snapchat itself has said in a press release, "We compete with other companies in every aspect of our business, particularly with companies that focus on mobile engagement and advertising. Many of these companies, such as Apple, Facebook (including Instagram and WhatsApp), Google (including YouTube), and Twitter, have significantly greater financial and human resources and, in some cases, larger user bases."

Apple? Facebook? Google? Those are three of the biggest and most successful tech companies in the world, and they are in direct competition with **upstart** Snapchat. Facebook's Instagram went head-on with Snapchat once again in August 2016 by launching Instagram Stories. Even Instagram CEO Kevin Systrom acknowledged that Snapchat deserved "all the credit" for creating the idea. However, Instagram seemed to be doing it right: in a very short time, more than 150 million people were using Instagram stories every day. A study conducted shortly after the Instagram Stories launch spelled bad news for Snapchat—it showed that daily active Snapchat user growth had slowed to a 5.3 percent rate, and the number of times Snapchat users accessed the app daily "declined significantly."

Another Facebook property, WhatsApp, is also a direct competitor. In February 2017, WhatsApp launched its own version of Stories, known as WhatsApp Status. The global messaging app already has over 1.2 billion users. That's an immense user base

Can internationally focused WhatsApp take market share from Snapchat?

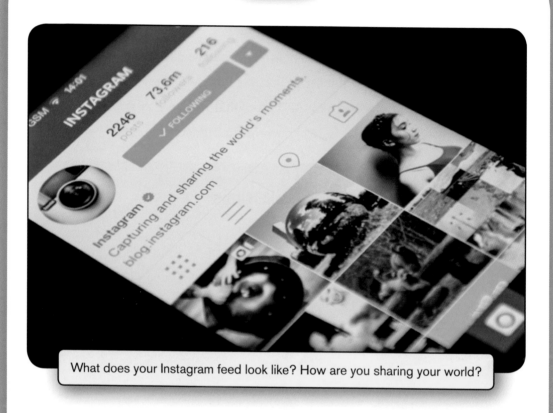

What does your Instagram feed look like? How are you sharing your world?

that's being exposed to something that acts and functions very much like Snapchat's own product.

The competition for Snapchat didn't begin with Instagram and WhatsApp, and it won't end with them either. Facebook is rumored to be rolling out its own version of Stories as well, possibly as a part of its Facebook News Feed or even attached to its own Messenger. Even Google, the company that hosts Snapchat with its cloud service, is said to be developing a competitor to Discover. All these developments, and many more, are ones to watch for Snapchat's users and lovers.

Whatever the outcome of the competition, though, Snapchat was the originator and the innovator. Now it's time to see if it's got the competitive flexibility to remain on top.

Text-Dependent Questions

1. What are some of the main competitors for Snapchat?

2. What were the results of Snapchat's IPO?

3. According to users, what is the most common type of content sent over Snapchat?

Research Project

Dig into the numbers behind Snapchat's history as a stock. What percentage of the company's shares was sold to the public in the IPO? What is the current stock price of the company, and how much are the two founders worth based on the amount of stock they hold?

FIND OUT MORE

Books

Baker, Benjamin. ***Understanding Snapchat: Explore the Definitive Guide to Using Snapchat.*** CreateSpace Independent Publishing Platform, 2017.

Case, Michael. ***Evan Spiegel: A Biography.*** CreateSpace Independent Publishing Platform, 2017.

Gallagher, Billy. ***How to Turn Down a Billion Dollars: The Snapchat Story.*** New York, NY: St. Martin's Press, 2018.

Peitz, Chelsea. ***Talking in Pictures: How Snapchat Changed Cameras, Communication, and Communities.*** CreateSpace Independent Publishing Platform, 2017.

Perry, Scott. ***Snapchat 101: Everything You Need to Know to Get Started on Snapchat.*** San Francisco, CA: Blurb, 2016.

Websites

Snapchat Homepage
https://www.snapchat.com/

Fortune Magazine: Snapchat: An Abridged History
http://fortune.com/2017/02/04/snapchat-abridged-history/

SERIES GLOSSARY OF KEY TERMS

algorithm a process designed for a computer to follow to accomplish a certain task

colleagues the people you work with

entrepreneurs people who start their own businesses, often taking financial risks to do so

incorporate sold shares of stock to become a publicly traded company

innovation creativity; the process of building something new

open-source describing a computer program that can be used by any programmer to create or modify the product

perks benefits to doing something

startups new companies just starting out.

targeting trying to reach a certain person or thing

venture capitalists people who invest money in young companies in hopes they will grow greatly in value

INDEX

Photo Credits

123RF: Tarapong Pattmachaiyant 28; Goodluz 47; Marcel de Grijs 59. CNBC: 15. Dreamstime.com: William Rodrigues Dos Santos 6; Dennizn 8, 20; Sagans1974 18; Dimarik16 21; Antonio Guillem 26; Ayo88 30; Yudesign 35; Lawrence Weslowski Jr. 36; Andre Durao 37; Aoleshko 40; Paul Pirosca 45; MBI 48; Raisa Kanareva 50; Vlue 52; Piotr Trojanowski 54; MrFly 60. Newscom: Monika Graff/UPI 57. Shutterstock: Debby Wong 10; Turtix 12; JRCpics 33.

About the Author

John Csiszar is a freelance writer and article curator. After graduating from UCLA, Csiszar was a registered investment advisor for 19 years before becoming a writer and editor. In addition to writing thousands of articles for online publications, including the Huffington Post, he has created, edited, and curated a variety of technology-oriented projects, from web pages and social media text to software help manuals. Csiszar lives in Hermosa Beach, California.